EARTH'S CYCLES

The Animal Life Cycle

CHERYL JAKAB

Smart Apple Media

Smart Apple Media
2140 Howard Drive West
North Mankato, Minnesota 56003

First published in 2007 by
MACMILLAN EDUCATION AUSTRALIA PTY LTD
627 Chapel Street, South Yarra, Australia 3141

Visit our Web site at www.macmillan.com.au or go directly to www.macmillanlibrary.com.au

Associated companies and representatives throughout the world.

Copyright © Cheryl Jakab 2007

Library of Congress Cataloging-in-Publication Data

Jakab, Cheryl.
  The animal life cycle / by Cheryl Jakab.
  p. cm. — (Earth's cycles)
  Includes index.
  ISBN 978-1-59920-148-1
  1. Animal life cycles—Juvenile literature. I. Title.

QL49.J25 2007
591.7—dc22

2007004558

Edited by Erin Richards
Text and cover design by Christine Deering
Page layout by Christine Deering
Photo research by Jes Senbergs
Illustrations by Ann Likhovetsky, pp. 13, 15, 17, 18.

Printed in U.S.

Acknowledgements
The author and the publisher are grateful to the following for permission to reproduce copyright material:

Front cover photographs: African elephants and calves (center), courtesy of Daryl Balfour/Getty Images; chicks (background), courtesy of Photodisc.

Arco Images/Alamy, p. 28 (top); Peter Arnold Inc/Alamy, p. 11; (top); Steve Bloom Images/Alamy, p. 5; Shaun Cunningham/Alamy, p. 26; Tim Graham/Alamy, p. 19; INSADCO Photography/Alamy, p. 15; mediacolor's/Alamy, p. 6; Natural Visions/Alamy, p. 14 (top); Greg Philpott/Alamy, p. 10 (bottom); Jack Cameron/ANTPhoto.com, p. 25; Jan Aldenhoven/Auscape, p. 10 (top); Bios/Auscape, p. 21 (bottom); Amy Shapiro/Auscape, p. 12; Dr David Wachenfeld/Auscape, p. 28 (bottom); Corbis, pp. 4 (middle right & top left); 20 (middle left & middle right) Daryl Balfour/Getty Images, pp. 1, 9, 23 (top); John Guistina/Getty Images, p. 22 (bottom); Charles Melton/Getty Images, p. 23 (bottom); Gunther Schmida/Lochman Transparencies, p. 14 (bottom); NASA, pp. 4, 30; Otto Pfister/ NHPA, p.16; Photodisc, pp. 4 (bottom left, bottom right, middle left & top right), 8, 13, 20 (bottom left, bottom right, center & top), 21 (top), 22 (top); Photolibrary, pp. 11 (bottom), 24; Photos.com, p. 7; John Reader / Science Photot Library, p. 27.

While every care has been taken to trace and acknowledge copyright, the publisher tenders their apologies for any accidental infringement where copyright has proved untraceable. Where the attempt has been unsuccessful, the publisher welcomes information that would redress the situation.

Contents

Baby

Egg   Young animal

Adult

ideas and tips

Glossary words
When a word is printed in **bold**, you can look up its meaning in the glossary on page 31.

Earth's natural cycles

What is a cycle?

A cycle is a never-ending series of changes that repeats again and again. Arrows in cycle diagrams show the direction in which the cycle is moving.

Earth's natural cycles create every environment on Earth. Living and non-living things are constantly changing. Each change is part of a natural cycle. Earth's natural cycles are working all the time.

Earth's non-living cycles are:
- the water cycle
- the rock cycle
- the seasons cycle

Earth's living cycles are:
- the food cycle
- the animal life cycle
- the plant life cycle

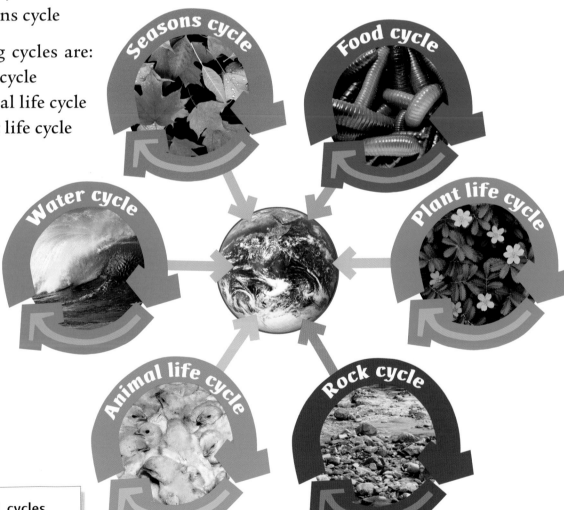

Earth's natural cycles keep the planet healthy.

The balance of nature

Earth's natural cycles all connect with each other. The way the cycles connect is sometimes called the balance of nature.

Keeping the balance

Every living thing depends on Earth's natural cycles to survive. A change in one cycle can affect the whole balance of nature. Knowing how Earth's cycles work helps us keep the environment healthy.

Every living thing depends on the balance of nature to survive.

5

Animals

The animal kingdom is divided into two main groups, **vertebrates** and **invertebrates**. Vertebrates include birds, fishes, **mammals**, reptiles, and frogs. Invertebrates include worms, snails, crabs, insects, and spiders.

Animals are living things that get their food by eating other living things. Animals are found in every **habitat** on Earth. They live on the land, in fresh water, and in the oceans. There are more than two million types of animals on Earth. Animals make up one of the five main kingdoms of living things. The other kingdoms are plants, fungi, **bacteria,** and single-celled life.

The praying mantis is an invertebrate that eats other animals.

The importance of animals

Animals are a very important part of the natural environment. Along with plants, animals help maintain every habitat on Earth.

Why are animals important to people?

Animals provide people with food, such as meat, fish, and eggs. Many people also enjoy the company of animals.

How do people affect animals?

People affect animals when they clear the land to make way for farms and homes. This loss of natural habitat threatens the survival of many animals.

How do animals fit into the balance of nature?

Animals eating and being eaten are a big part of the balance of nature. Animals change the surface of the land by moving about, digging burrows, and building their homes.

Polar bears are an important part of the Arctic habitat.

The animal life cycle

The animal life cycle shows the different stages that occur in the life of an animal. It shows how each baby animal starts life and grows up to become an adult. The life cycle also shows how the next generation of animals is produced.

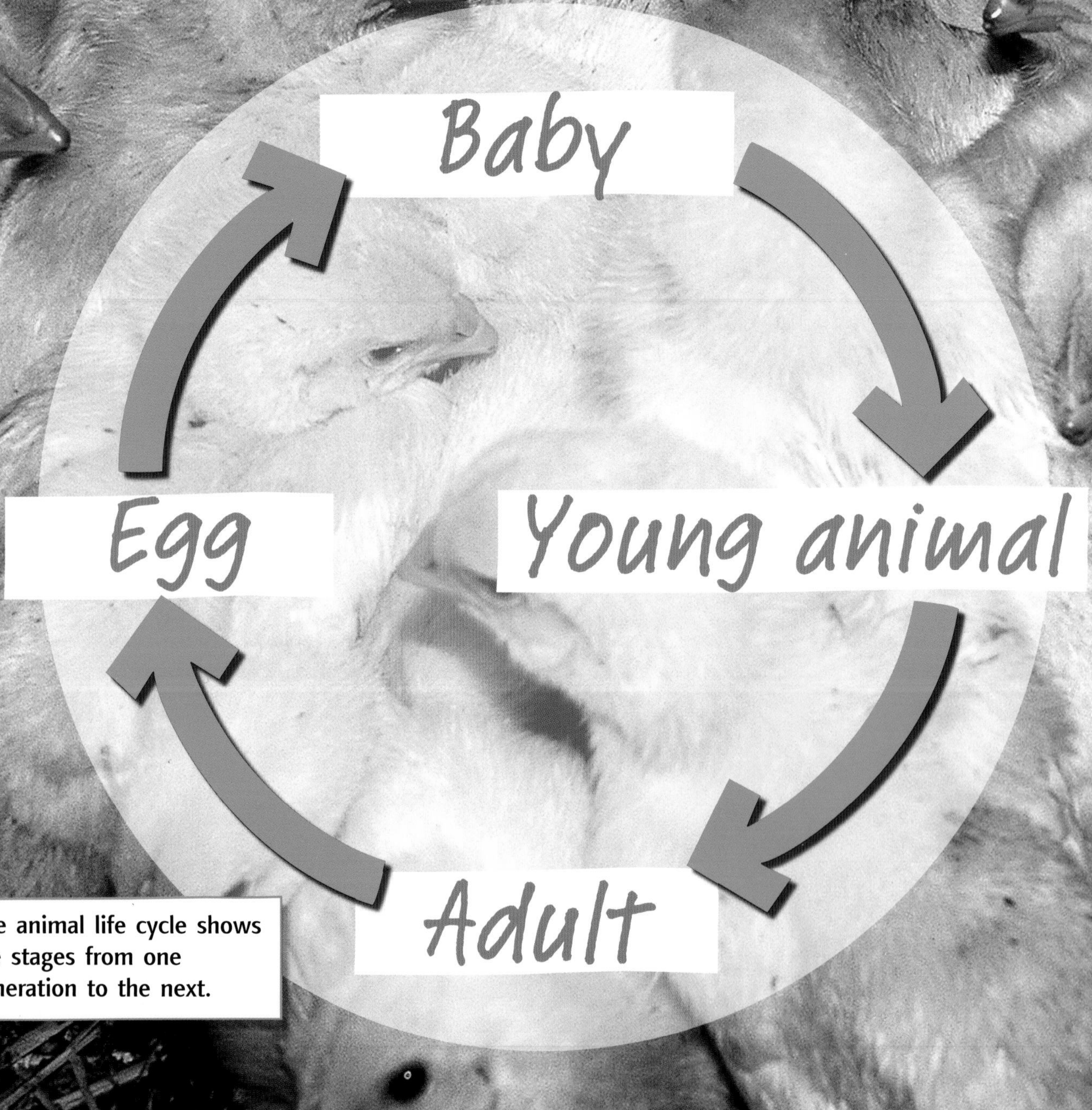

Baby

Young animal

Adult

Egg

The animal life cycle shows the stages from one generation to the next.

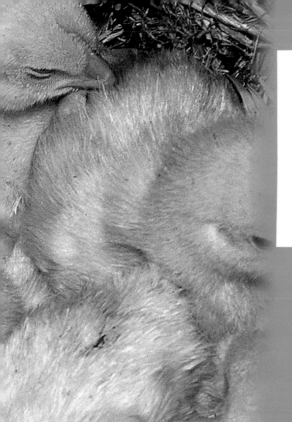

Different life cycles

Different animals can have very different life cycles. The changes animals go through at each stage of the cycle can be very different. How long it takes to complete each stage, and the life span of an animal, depends on the **species**.

Elephants have a life span of more than sixty years.

Baby

The first stage in life for each animal is as a baby. A baby animal is either born or hatched from an egg. Being born is when a baby separates from its mother. Most mammal babies develop inside the mother and are then born. A few frog, reptile, and insect babies are also born.

Most animals are not born, but hatch from eggs that have been laid. This includes birds, fishes, spiders, insects, and most reptiles and frogs

Baby crocodiles hatch from eggs that were laid by their mother.

Baby horses, called foals, develop inside the mother and are born.

10

Care by parents

Some baby animals are fed and cared for by their parents. This also helps them learn from their parents. Many mammals, such as humans, gorillas, and whales, care for their babies for a very long time. Other animals, such as snails and other invertebrates, lay huge numbers of eggs at one time. The baby animals are often left to take care of themselves.

Gorillas look after their babies for a long time after birth.

Young animal

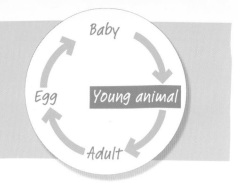
In the next stage of the life cycle, a baby becomes a growing young animal. As a young animal grows, its body goes through many changes. The behavior of a young animal also changes as it grows.

Change in size

For young animals that look like their parents, growing up is mainly about getting bigger. Young horses look just like their parents when they are born, only much smaller. For these young animals, this growing stage is slow and gradual.

Many young animals, such as bear cubs, look like tiny versions of their parents.

12

Change in appearance

Some young animals do not look like their parents at all. Tadpoles are young frogs, but do not look like fully-grown frogs. Caterpillars hatch from butterfly eggs, but do not have wings and cannot fly. They do not look like their parents at all. These animals make big changes in the way they look as they grow.

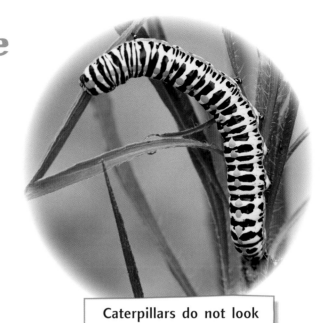

Caterpillars do not look like butterflies when they are young.

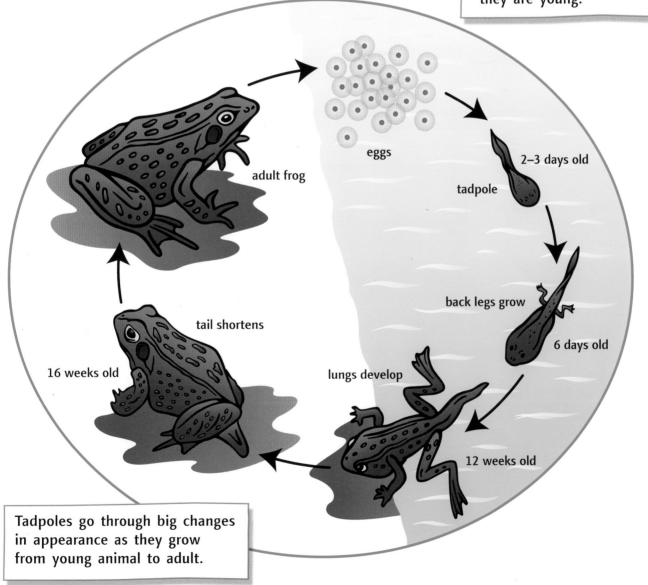

eggs

2–3 days old

tadpole

back legs grow

6 days old

adult frog

tail shortens

16 weeks old

lungs develop

12 weeks old

Tadpoles go through big changes in appearance as they grow from young animal to adult.

Adult

A young animal grows up to become an adult in the next stage of the life cycle. An animal is an adult when it is fully grown and able to reproduce. Many insects reach adulthood after only a few weeks. Larger animals can take many years to become adults.

Male and female

Most animal species have male and female adults. Male and female adults often look similar, although often male vertebrates are larger. In some animal species, the adult male looks very different from the adult female.

Male and female adult tigers look like each other.

The adult male bowerbird is much more colorful than the female.

Metamorphosis

To become adults, some animals change their shape completely. This rapid change from the young animal is called metamorphosis. Metamorphosis may take place inside a cocoon, such as when a caterpillar changes into a butterfly.

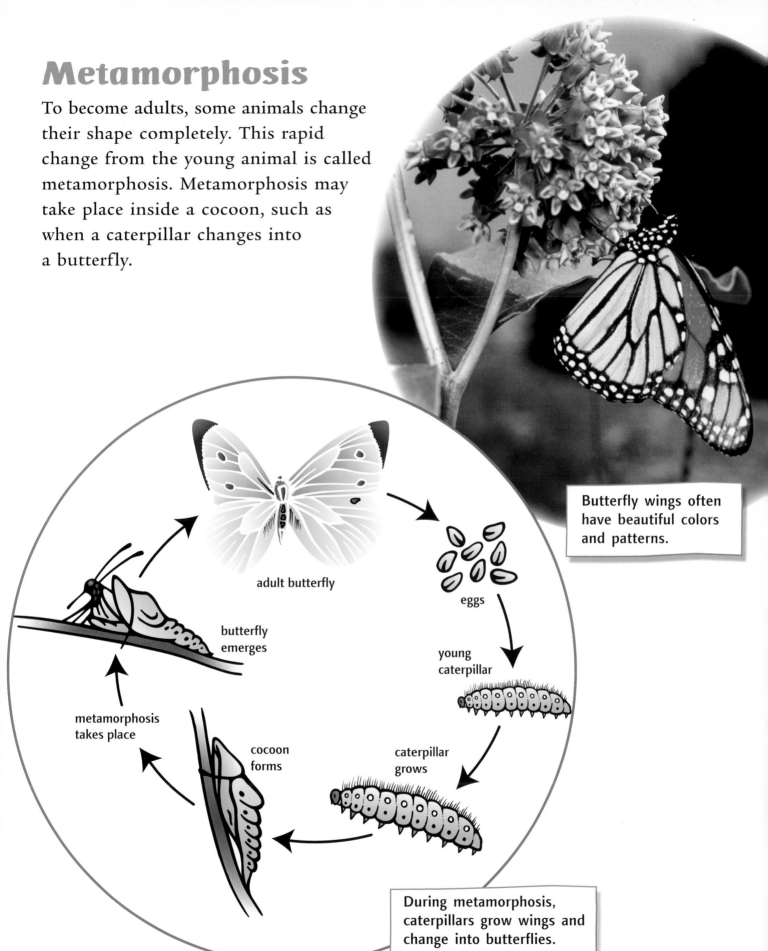

adult butterfly

butterfly emerges

metamorphosis takes place

cocoon forms

eggs

young caterpillar

caterpillar grows

Butterfly wings often have beautiful colors and patterns.

During metamorphosis, caterpillars grow wings and change into butterflies.

Egg

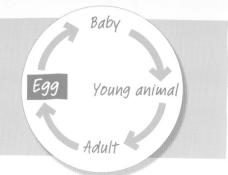

Once an animal becomes a fully mature adult, it can reproduce. This is what happens in the next stage of the animal life cycle. Most animals reproduce sexually. An adult male mates with an adult female to **fertilize** an egg. Some animals, such as sponges, can reproduce **asexually** by budding or breaking pieces off.

Courtship

Courtship brings males and females together to mate. Courting rituals can be complex and lengthy. Many birds dance and sing together, just as humans may do when courting. In many bird species, the colorful feathers of the male attract the female.

A peacock displays his colorful feathers to attract a peahen.

Mating

Mating is the process of female eggs being fertilized by male **sperm**. Many water animals, such as some mollusks and fish, fertilize their eggs in the water. Other animals fertilize the eggs inside the body of the female.

The fertilized egg

Most animals begin as a tiny fertilized egg cell. When an egg cell is fertilized, it can develop into a new baby animal. Whether inside an egg or inside the female, the developing baby is called an **embryo**.

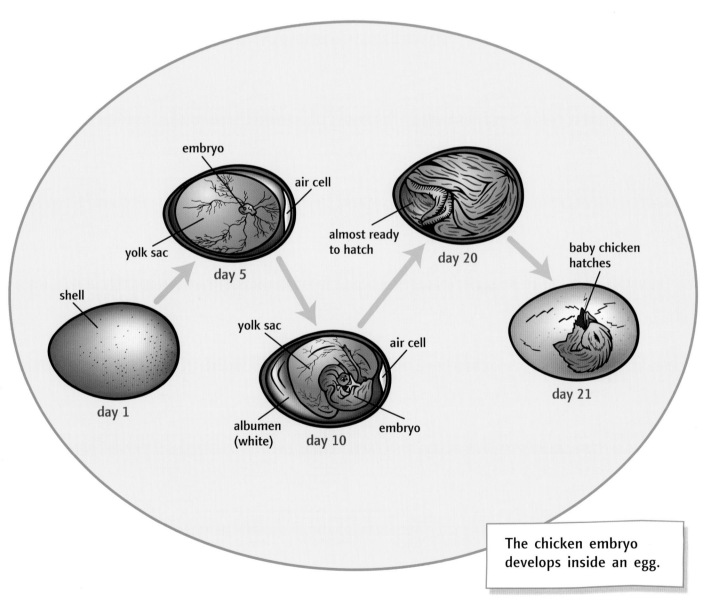

embryo

air cell

yolk sac

day 5

shell

day 1

yolk sac

albumen (white)

air cell

embryo

day 10

almost ready to hatch

day 20

baby chicken hatches

day 21

The chicken embryo develops inside an egg.

Animal life span

What is a life span?

Animals are born or hatch, live and grow for a certain length of time, and then die. This is called the life span of the animal. Each animal species has a different life span. Dying is also part of the animal life cycle.

Different animals have different life spans. Most mammals have a life span of less than 20 years. Elephants and whales can live for more than 60 years. Larger animals usually live longer than smaller animals, but not always. Many insects, such as the mayfly, live for only one day.

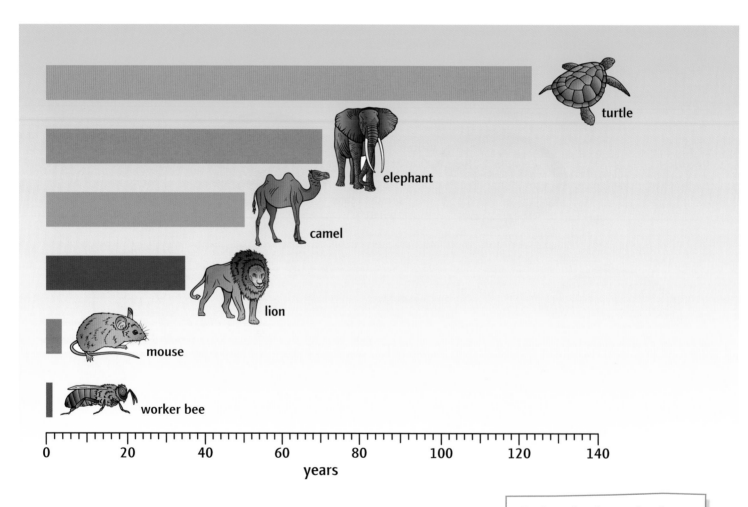

turtle

elephant

camel

lion

mouse

worker bee

0   20   40   60   80   100   120   140

years

Each animal species has its own average life span.

Death

Death is the end stage of life for all living things. Death can happen at any stage of the animal life cycle. Many babies and young animals do not live to adulthood. Some are killed by **predators**, while others catch diseases or have accidents. An animal may die as a baby, a young animal, an adult, or in old age.

Vultures are scavengers that feed on dead animals.

What happens to dead bodies?
After death, animal bodies are recycled back into the environment. The dead body may be eaten by **scavengers**, or become food for **decomposers**, such as worms, bacteria, and fungi. Decomposers cause dead bodies to rot, or decompose, releasing **nutrients** into the soil. This is how animal bodies are recycled back into the soil.

The balance of nature

The balance of nature shows how the animal life cycle is linked with Earth's other cycles. Animals have an effect on non-living and living things in every environment. The seasons, food, plants, rocks, and water all help to maintain the animal life cycle.

The animal life cycle is an important part of the balance of nature.

Animals and the seasons

Seasons trigger animal activities, including courting, mating, and egg laying. Some animals, such as bears, **hibernate** in winter. Many animals **migrate** from one place to another according to the season.

As the seasons change, many birds migrate to other parts of the world to find food.

Animals, rocks, and soil

Animals are active creatures that can change the land. Many small animals, such as worms, live in and help form the soil. Many animals dig into the soil for protection, to nest, or to find food. Small animals, such as meerkats, make big changes to rocks and soil when building their homes.

Meerkats make their homes in rocks and soil.

21

Animals and water

Water is very important to animals. All animals need water to survive.

Water animals

Many animals spend their whole lives in the rivers, lakes and oceans on Earth. Animals that live in water include fish, corals, crabs and octopuses. Some mammals, including whales and dolphins, also live in water. Frogs spend part of their lives in water and part of their lives on land.

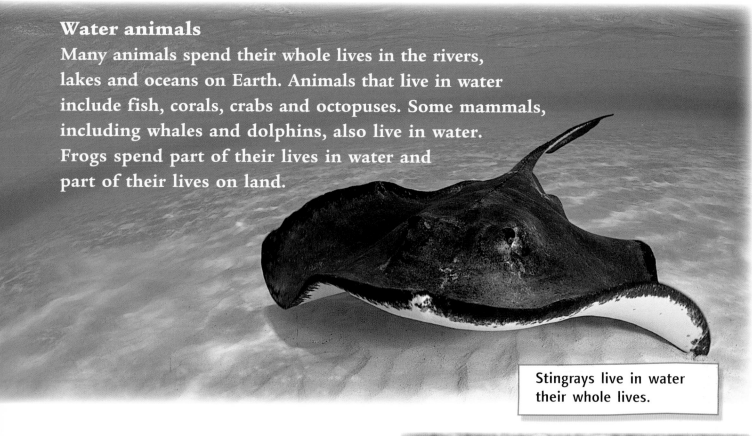

Stingrays live in water their whole lives.

Land animals

Land animals need fresh water to drink. Without fresh water, most land animals cannot survive. Many animals travel long distances to find fresh water in rivers, lakes, and waterholes.

Elephants cannot survive without fresh water.

Animals and food

The availability of food has a big effect on animal numbers. When food is in short supply, many animals do not reproduce. They use all their energy to make sure they survive. When there is plenty of plant food, plant-eating animals produce young. More plant-eating animals means a good food supply for meat-eating animals, and improves their chances of survival.

Animals and plants

Plants often rely on animals to fertilize them and to spread their seeds. This helps plants reproduce and grow in new areas. Plants also provide food for plant-eating animals.

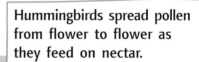

Hummingbirds spread pollen from flower to flower as they feed on nectar.

People and animals

People use animals in many different ways. Farm animals, such as cows, sheep, pigs, goats, and chickens, are used for food and for clothes that people wear. Many people also enjoy keeping animals as pets. However, many animal species are **endangered** because of human activities, such as land-clearing, overfishing, and introduced species.

Habitat destruction is a major threat to the survival of many animals.

Land-clearing

People have cleared huge areas of land that were once rich habitat for animals. Cities, towns, and farms now cover areas that were once natural habitats. Land-clearing is a major threat to many animals. It removes the things they depend on, such as food and shelter. Most animals cannot continue their life cycles without natural habitat.

Overfishing

Many fish in Earth's oceans and rivers are threatened by overfishing. Overfishing is when people catch fish faster than the fish can reproduce. Overfishing in oceans and rivers has endangered many fish species.

Introduced species

Introduced species are animals that are taken by people to places where they do not naturally live. They can increase in number quickly and become pests in the new environment. Rabbits introduced to Australia and the common starling introduced to the United States are now pests.

Rabbits introduced to Australia are damaging the environment.

Animal conservation

Animal conservation is the process of protecting animals so they can survive. It means people thinking about the needs of animals before carrying out certain activities. Today, there are more than 6,000 endangered animal species on Earth. It is estimated that 50 to 100 species become **extinct** every day. Conservation includes keeping some natural habitat for each species. Some endangered species are also **bred in captivity** to stop them from dying out.

The whooping crane is bred in captivity to keep it from dying out.

Trade in ivory from elephant tusks is now illegal.

Trade in animal products

People buying and selling animal products is a major threat to many animals. Trade in hides, feathers, horns, and tusks has endangered many animal species. CITES is the Convention on International Trade in Endangered Species of Wild Fauna and Flora. It is an international agreement designed to protect endangered wildlife. The CITES agreement makes trade in endangered species illegal, and has been signed by 51 nations.

Protecting animals

Everyone can help protect animals. Getting active can help save animals and maintain the balance of nature.

Get active

- Find out about endangered species in your area
- Join a local conservation group
- Read the labels on the food you buy (is your canned tuna dolphin-friendly?)
- Grow plants that feed and protect local birds, lizards, frogs, and insects
- Stop pet dogs and cats from hunting and killing local wildlife

Pet cats will hunt if they get the chance.

Conservation groups work to protect endangered animals, such as sea turtles.

Research an endangered animal

Do some research on an endangered animal. Present your report to the class.

1 Choose an endangered animal in your local area or country to research.

2 Find out about its life cycle and life span. What habitat does it live in? What food does it eat?

3 Find out what has caused the animal to become endangered. Are the causes natural or are people changing its habitat? List the human activities.

4 How are people working to help save the endangered animal? Are there breeding programs? Are people protecting its natural habitat?

5 Present a report to the class. You could make a poster or do a presentation on a computer. You could even make a speech about the animal.

Living with nature

We all depend on the balance of nature for our survival. If people continue to disturb Earth's cycles, it will upset the balance of nature. Understanding Earth's cycles helps us care for Earth and live in harmony with nature.

"The Earth does not belong to us: we belong to the Earth."

(Chief Seattle Suquamish leader, about 1854)

Glossary

asexually	without female and male parts
bacteria	microscopic decomposers
bred in captivity	kept in a zoo and helped to reproduce
decomposers	living things that break down plant and animal material
embryo	a developing baby, before it is hatched or born
endangered	in danger of dying out
extinct	no longer existing
fertilize	to join an egg cell with sperm
habitat	place where plants and animals naturally live and grow
hibernate	sleep through winter to save energy
invertebrates	animals without backbones
mammals	animals that produce milk to feed their babies
migrate	move from one place to another
nutrients	substances that give living things energy to live and grow
predators	animals that catch, kill, and eat other animals
scavengers	animals that eat the flesh of already dead animals
species	a particular type of animal or plant
sperm	male reproductive cell

Index